Sketches of Venice

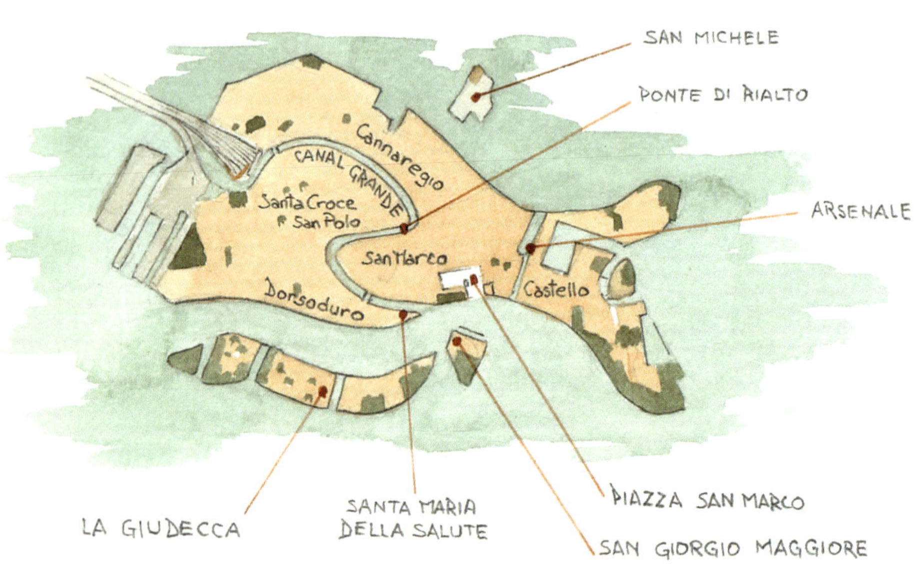

La Massane
Les Joncades Basses
13210 Saint-Remy-de-Provence

ISBN : 2 84135 496 2

Translated by: Mary Podevin

Sketches of Venice

Michel Duvoisin

ÉQUINOXE

"So great is the fame of this antique queen of the seas that it conjures up images of a vast city with immense palaces. Thus we are surprised that everything is small, small, small ! Venice is nothing but a curio, a trinket, an old, charming arty trinket, poor, ruined, but proud with a splendid pride of "past glory". Everything is in ruin, everything seems to be on the verge of collapsing into the water which props up the worn old city. Time has wreaked havoc on the palace fronts, stained with moisture, ravaged by the leprosy which eats away at the stone and marble. Some palace buildings vaguely list to one side, ready to fall, tired of having stood for so long on their pilings.

Suddenly the horizon opens, the lagoon widens. Over there on the right covered islands appear, and on the left, an admirable monument of Moorish style, full of Oriental grace and impressive elegance – the Doges Palace.

I will not tell of the Venice that everyone speaks about. Saint Mark's square resembles Palais-Royal square, Saint Mark's façade looks like a cardboard setting for a café-concert. But inside is the most absolute beauty one could imagine. The penetrating harmony of the lines and the shades, the reflections of the softened brilliance of the old gold in the mosaics set amidst severe marble, the splendid proportions of the vaulted ceilings and the distances, the indescribable something that comes from the whole, the quiet influx of daylight that becomes religious as it settles around the pillars, the sensations the eyes transmit to the spirit ... all make Saint Mark's the most completely admirable entity in the world.

But in contemplating this incomparable masterpiece of Byzantine art, the mind wanders, comparing it to another religious monument, itself also unrivalled, yet so different, a masterpiece of Gothic art, built amidst the waters, the gray waters of the northern seas. The mind's eye turns to the colossal granite jewel which stands alone in the immense Mont-Saint-Michel bay."

Guy de Maupassant,
in *Gil-Blas*,
Paris, 5 May
1885.

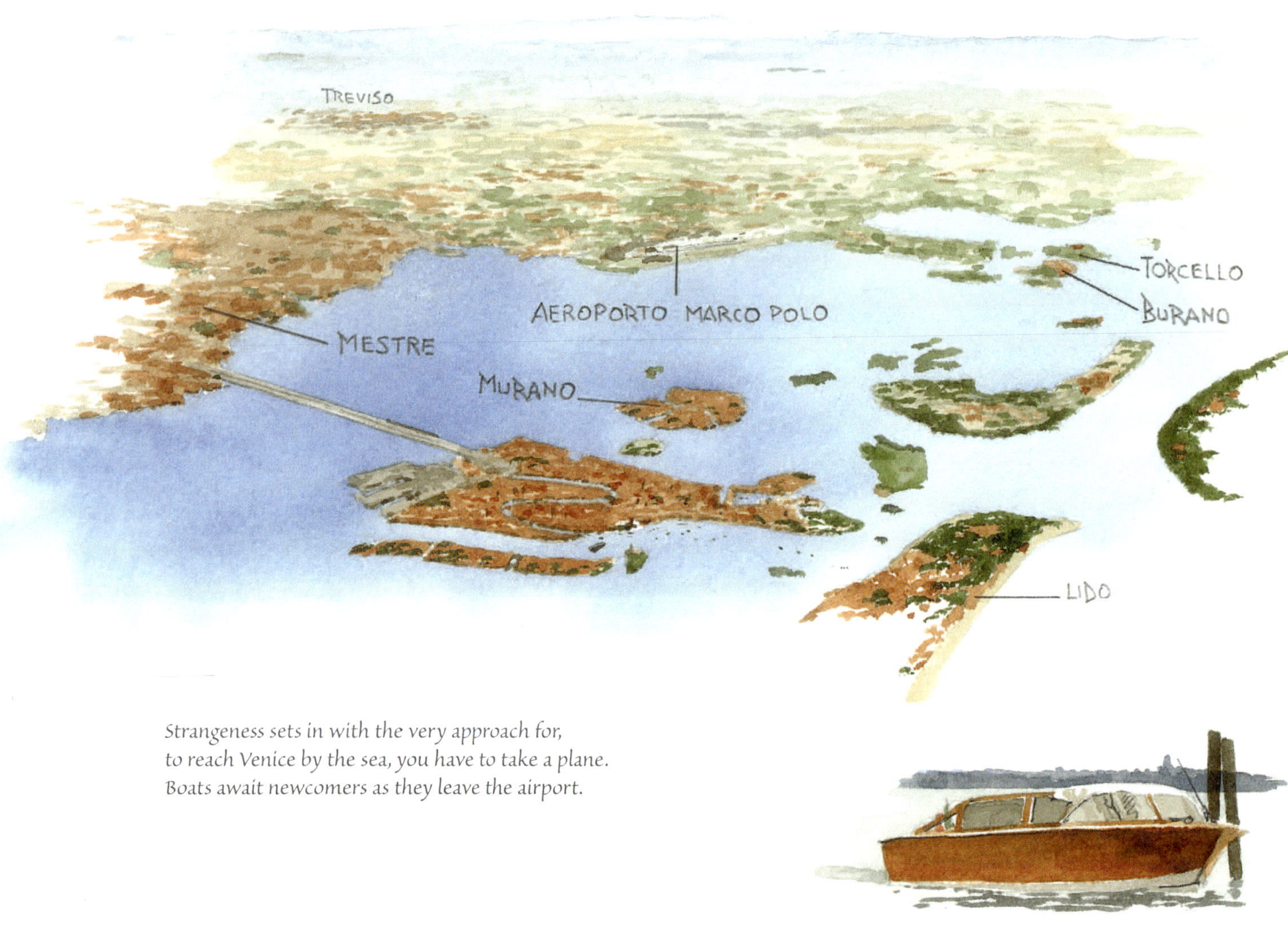

Strangeness sets in with the very approach for,
to reach Venice by the sea, you have to take a plane.
Boats await newcomers as they leave the airport.

On the left, the flat roof is Torcello. Burano lies to the right.

An enigmatic home on its tiny island between the airport and Venice.

Venice raises and waves its bell-towerarms to welcome new arrivals.

On the north bank, the line of palaces gives way to the Arsenal buildings. But all this is the other side of the picture. The extraordinary symphony awaits us on the other side of the island.

We have just to go around it, and unbelievable magic takes hold of our heart.

Majestic adagio which brings tears to our eyes and
strangles words in our throats.
Eternal vista that we think we've always known yet
which we rediscover anew each time with
amazement we didn't think possible.
This is Venice !

Campo della Maddalena.
The first vision we have as we stroll Venice.
A humble square and a well, amidst rose-colored homes and green rio,
similar to a thousand others.
And, like the others, unique.

Regardless of where you are, what you do, the peaceful winding streets come out on the Canal Grande.

Rio Trapolin

Rio dei Miracoli, a gondolier
awaits new clients.

Campo San Stefano
"A morning rain doesn't keep the artist indoors"
says the old Venetian proverb I just invented.

Despite what I may say otherwise,
the Piazza San Marco
will always be the unforgettable heart
of the heart of Venice.

In front of the Giardini ex Reali,
the traveler comes to find the souvenir which remains,
the irrefutable testimony to his brief passage.

San Giorgio Maggiore.

Rio San Felice opens onto
Canal Grande opposite
Casa Favretto.

Here's the Venice I love
walking through and sketching.
Venice is a rio, a square, a well,
a stairway, a red-brick wall
with a white stone festoon.
Better yet, it's a soul, ghosts
which wander here and there,
the echo of voices in total unison
with the place.
Steps which resonate off
the marble slabs paving the street.
But Venice is also, and perhaps above all,
peace and silence.

Let's discover some splendid spots
without saying a word,
just by turning the pages …

See !
No need for words to fall in love with Venice.
The explanation "we love Venice" totally suffices.

Just a few stone throws from Venice,
Murano and its glass-making studios
come to life.

Here the Canal Grande has taken on the shape of a snake, and its delicious venom, actually a beneficial philter, circulates throughout.
How could anyone resist so much beauty ?

Each palace has its own tale to tell,
of a flamboyant civilization which
continues to strive each day to retain
its panache.

Stone parapet or wrought
iron balustrades, this bridge settles
the question in its own way.
But watch out if you cross it
when you've had a bit
too much Valpolicello !

Rio
San Felice

Steps away from the Bridge of Sighs where crowds gather,
Sant'Apollon cloister is a secret oasis of silence and cool serenity.

Rio di San Paolo.

Rio Terra Antonio Foscarini.
Painting this small trattoria terrace has whetted my appetite.
Hmmm ! Farfalle e seppie all'inchiostro !

The garden lining the Canal Grande beckons to the Casanovas of the moment, enticing them into its shade.

All I could draw of the Arsenal is the beauty of the main entrance,
for beyond is military terrain.

Campiello Querini

Early morning facing rio San Vidal. Just to the right,
Accademia bridge does not yet have to convey the hosts of visitors.

Campo San Maurizio and another
balcony for another Juliette.

Two drawings of rio San Provolo,
each seen from the other's bridge.

Rio San Giuseppe.

Somewhat far from the post cards, but the adventurous soul is highly rewarded.
Today I didn't see a single tourist.

Campo dei Gesuiti
in the Cannaregio area
is a Verdi setting come to life.

Café Florian.

Wherever you sit,
you are in a work by Canaletto, Bellini, Guardi,
Hemingway or any one of countless other artists.
The past here is as heavy as the present is delicious.

Rio di Palazzo della Paglia

The Bridge of Sighs.
A universal legend that needs no introduction,
but at this time of night you can hear them.

Rio della Serisa
Undoubtedly built for lovers to stop and kiss . . .

and, on Canal Grande, a romantic terrace for them to dine by candlelight.

Between the lagoon and the Piazza,
the Piazzetta offers countless details
each of which deserves a lengthy gaze.

Rio della Frescada

and rio dei Frari,
in the heart
of the maze.

Strange, supernatural vision where the sun plays with the rain above the marbled water opposite the Guidecca.
Storms threaten, one invokes the protection of the "della Spirito Santo" and of the covered porch to his church.

A gondola ride is for two people only,
nestled in each other's arms.
If possible, far from the crowds.
Silence reigns,
perhaps the notes of a barcarolle.
No running commentary –
this is no guided visit !
A gondola ride is unreal and timeless,
flowing with the water,
shimmering with love.

*You can't miss this bridge
on the rio de Torreselle
if you're going to la Salute.*

Rio di Santa Maria Formosa,
rio and calle del Paradiso,
fondamenta dei Preti and
rio del Piombo come together
here in an inextricable imbroglio.

San Michele.
Island, cemetery, garden, book of memories where each page holds a famous name.

Campiello Barbaro.
We were here three pages ago.

Crowds in Venice ? Yes, sometimes.
But it's easy to find yourself alone in the labyrinth of the old narrow streets.

The ungainly vaporetti
are part of the landscape.
You get used to them.
You even end up truly liking them.
The "stazione" are there . . .
we'd like a little more time . . .

Ah ! The pomodori,
the fagioli, the carciofi selected by Angelo !

As for the big market
near the Rialto –
sheer splendor !

Rio Terra dei Catecumeni

A rio terra is a canal which has been filled in once and for all.

Rio dei Greci

All the bell-towers lean just a bit,
to the left or right, sometimes,
it seems, to both sides.
Even the police can do
nothing about it.

Rio dei Santissimo di San Stefano. Rio di Santa Maria.
In a long-ago drawing class, I learned that
vertical lines give a feeling of calm.
What a beautiful restful day !

Fondamenta Rimpetto.

The streetlamps near San Moise
are a daily celebration.

Enticing, exuberant exciting Burano
talks too loud and wears too much makeup.
Sparkling, amorous, lascivious Burano.
Spellbinding Burano, decked out in lace,
sings in the sun drawing in all the passers-by.

Rio di Ca Moro.
This is near … where I do not know. I'm lost.

Today, I'm drawn to the Canal Grande. I feel like space, that's all!

San Pietro, from one end to the other.
A Venetian isle for Venetians.
Travelers don't have the time … or the legs,
to come out here.

In the Dorsudoro area,
each step you take
deserves to be sketched.

Squero San Trovaso

Here like elsewhere, time has stood still,
the shipyards and the gondolas they make haven't changed.

Up to the first bridge,
this is the Fondamenta Zen. After, it's another.

A mouse hole ? Cat door ?
Hidden door for unfaithful
sailors plying their wares ?

To detect beauty in all this you undoubtedly have to be a painter, know how to pare down, sort, interpret, extract the pathos and transform it into a poem.

Rio de Torreselle. Ah !
Venice, Venice !
How not to love you ?

The soul of Venice is found in the details, these worn renderings, these old walls of stone caressed by the water, decrepit doors which have seen high water.

Rio San Lorenzo

Disrespectful pigeons on Goldoni's hat.
Is nothing sacred ?!

Campo di San Polo.

No rio flows here but the shade is refreshingly cool. I'm eager to finish my morning tasks to then sit under the spacious parasols and enjoy "spaghetti alle vongole".

A bric-a-brac of brick and stone.

Here there's green, white and red. Is this a lavish garden or a sumptuous flag?

Palazzo da Mula on Murano.
Perhaps a former convent or simply
the palace gardens.

Rio Prieili,
Totally conducive to dreaming.

The view from the top of Scala del Bovolo
requires climbing several steps,
but the reward is more than worth it.

Corte Bottera

Omnipresent wells,
humble or opulent, are all rainwater wells which were wells of life.

Rio della Salute, where leafy terraces grow cool and fresh as dusk falls.

From the vaporetto station, a single road leads to the charming small village of Torcello, clustered around its cathedral, Santa Maria Assunta, almost too big for it, and its church, Santa Fosca.

Like a vessel cleaving the waters of the lagoon,
Santa Maria della Salute brandishes its
Dogana di Mare like a figurehead.

Does not overall beauty come down to
the exquisiteness of each detail ?

*It's not true ! I do think of other things than food . . . but I have to admit,
a splendid plate of fettucine in salsa and a glass of Valpolicella,
gazing out over the Lido makes for a nice break !*

Would I have loved you Venice in your youth,
at the time of your sparkling beauty,
when you lived extravagantly,
masquerading half the year to forget life ?
Would I have loved you Venice,
if I had been twenty the day we met ?
Would I have understood your majesty,
the majesty we see in the eyes of a beautiful woman
halfway through her life ?
Regardless, even if I had only met you today,
you are as I see you,
and that is how you seduced me.

Rio della Guerra

In Burano, building painters
are anything but subtle.

Humble Mazzorbo leaves the showing off to Burano.

Giardini Garibaldi,
a soldier perpetuates
the position.

Burano seen from Mazzorbo. And if the tower doesn't look straight, that's because it isn't straight. Period.

San Giorgio wanted
to be on my drawing
so of course
I included it.

Twilight, the end of the day. A sense of calm pervades Venice as it prepares to go out for the evening.

Far from Venice and its prestigious buildings,
the gentle countryside of Torcello
is restful and reviving.

The lovely San Francesco della Vignes cloister is absolute calm, which means it is very far from the city center.

Rio della Panada
Behind me is the lagoon and San Michele island,
but I preferred to draw the lively center of the city.

Just felt like coming back to San Pietro.

The rain had to come. Sheltered by the Procuratie Nuove, the passers-by tarry over my work.
Their critical eye gives way to smiles of admiration, or perhaps compassion.

Palazzo Contarini
This spiral staircase is particularly hard to grasp.

Campo San Zaccaria

The ultra-famous Rialto bridge
must excuse me for having drawn its portrait so late,
as if I had overlooked it and hasten to make amends.

The Campo delle Gorne
Looks like a village square with children playing and the elders chatting.

The rio della Sensa winds before my eyes, seemingly in the middle of the water, like a gondola.

Rio dell'Orso in both cool shade and bright light.

San Giorgio raises its arms as if
saying goodbye.

These two details symbolize all the forgotten beauties,
but no one ever has enough time in Venice.
An entire life wouldn't be long enough to paint it all.

Rio di San Stin

My last rio before who knows when. My pencil hesitates, my brush struggles. Like each time, I arrived a "Parisian in Venice", and in just a few days, will feel like a Venetian émigré, with but one desire, to come back as soon as I can.

My sketchbook is full and closes like the last rays of sun over Salute end the day.

I dreamed of filling these pages and now the work is done and has become reality.

Like a photograph of a loved one has to make up for his or her absence, so these pages of watercolors will help me wait until I can return to Venice once again.

I hope that in leafing through this little book, you will, like I do, sense the same sensations and hear the same songs of the faraway gondolier, in our imagination…

Printed in June 2005
on the Grafiche Zanini printing presses in Bologna, Italy
Photoengraving: Quadriscan, in Oraison

Layout by the author
Cover by Étienne Marie